TECHNOLOGY: BLUEPRINTS OF THE FUTURE™

TECHNOLOGY:
BLUEPRINTS OF THE FUTURE™

Super Jumbo Jets

Inside and Out

by

Holly Cefrey

Illustrations

Alessandro Bartolozzi

Leonello Calvetti, Lorenzo Cecchi

The Rosen Publishing Group's
PowerPlus Books™
New York

Dedicated to W.W.II Glider Pilot Theodore Cefrey

Published in 2002 in North America
by The Rosen Publishing Group, Inc., New York

First Edition

Book Design:
Andrea Dué s.r.l. Florence, Italy

Illustrations:
Alessandro Bartolozzi, Leonello Calvetti, Lorenzo Cecchi

Editor and Photo Researcher:
Joanne Randolph

Library of Congress Cataloging-in-Publication Data

Cefrey, Holly.
Super jumbo jets : inside and out / by Holly Cefrey. — 1st ed.
p. cm. — (Technology—blueprints of the future)
Includes bibliographical references and index.
Contents: To super jumbo, or not to super jumbo? - A Competition - Try, try again: humans in flight - Old rivalry, new planes - The Concorde - Forces of flight - The Airbus A380 - Jet engines: masters of thrust - Turbofan power - Looking inside a turbofan - Airbus cutaway - The jumbo generation - An international project - Construction - Super jumbo design - High-tech materials - Interiors - The future - Major Airlines of the World.
ISBN 0-8239-6112-5 (library binding)
1. Jet transports—Juvenile literature. [1. Jet transports. 2. Jet transports.]
I. Title. II. Series.
TK685.7 .C44 2002
629.133'349—dc21
2002001744
Manufactured in Italy by Eurolitho S.p.A., Milan

Contents

To Super Jumbo or not to Super Jumbo?

Today, the sound of airplanes flying overhead is a familiar one. We have grown accustomed to planning trips in terms of hours rather than days, as we did in the days before commercial airline travel was a possibility for regular people. Flight has always been a dream of humankind, since Leonardo da Vinci designed a set of wings to be worn by a person and even before that. However, it has taken technological advances to make that dream a reality. Many people have contributed their ideas and knowledge to make this a safe transportation alternative. Commercial airliners have spent a lot of time and energy since then trying to affordably bring this possibility to as many people as possible. The size of airliners has grown by leaps and bounds. Airlines are continually trying to figure out how to get more people in the air, whether it be through more flights or through larger planes. The creation of a jumbo jet was a big step toward this goal. Not only did it allow airlines to transport more people, but it also opened new possibilities for shipping cargo. Even the space shuttle took a ride on a jumbo jet!

The latest question in the world of commercial aviation is whether bigger or faster planes are the way to meet travelers' demands. Both methods mean new technologies are needed to design new planes. Every time new technology surfaces in aviation, one of the biggest challenges is convincing travelers that the plane is safe. Despite these challenges a new super jumbo jet is being created by Airbus, and a plane that travels close to the speed of sound is in development by Boeing. Will there be enough people who want to travel by air to fill such big planes? Will people feel confident enough in the safety of a super-fast jet to take advantage of it? Only time will tell whether super jumbo jets or jets that cut down flying time are the wave of the future. Time will also tell what new technologies will bring to the world of flight. Where do you think the future of jumbo jets lies?

Below: In 1977, a modified Boeing 747 was delivered to NASA for use as the delivery vehicle of the space shuttle.

Left: A Boeing 747 takes British Airways passengers to their destination. British Airways operates three versions of the Boeing 747: the series 400, 200 and 100. The airline operates 57 Boeing 747-400s including the new 747-400 Light Weight (Lite) aircraft. The 200 series are retired.

Below: A Boeing 747 is nearing completion in the Boeing warehouse.

A Competition

Airplanes make it possible for us to travel great distances in just a matter of hours. Jet airplanes, which include supersonic jets and jumbo jets, are the latest and the fastest means of air travel.

Supersonic jets travel faster than the speed of sound. Think about when you snap your fingers. The sound of the snap travels to your ear almost instantly. The time that it takes the sound to travel from your finger to your ear is the speed of sound. Supersonic jets travel faster than the time it takes for you to hear your fingers snap. Supersonic jets have limits though. The number of passengers that these fast jets can carry is much less than the number that jumbo jets can carry. Supersonic jets are also very loud. This level of noise can be unhealthy for human ears.

Jumbo jets are large planes that take many passengers over great distances. Various plane builders make jumbo jets. The planes are sold to airline companies throughout the world. Airline companies such as Virgin, Air France, American, Lufthansa, Japan Airlines, and Singapore Airlines use jumbo jets. The airline companies use jumbo jets to deliver thousands of people to various destinations daily.

Above: Planes have grown in size a lot. Notice how large the Boeing 747 (the gray drawing) is when compared to the Boeing 707 (the dark silhouette).

Just one of these big planes can carry more than 400 passengers in a single trip. Airline companies like this because having more passengers can mean more money for the company. Airline companies can get more passengers to their destinations by using bigger planes.

Over the next few years, jet planes are expected to get even bigger and better than the planes we have today. Two major jet plane builders are in a race to build the largest and fastest passenger planes ever. These companies are Airbus Industrie and the Boeing Company. Airbus is based in Europe, and Boeing is based in America.

Both companies have very different ideas about the future of air travel, or aviation. Airbus Industrie believes that the future lies in planes that are much larger than the jumbo jet. Boeing believes that the future lies in faster planes, which would cut down on travel time. The competition between Airbus Industrie and Boeing will lead to new and awesome planes, including larger, faster, and increasingly high-tech planes.

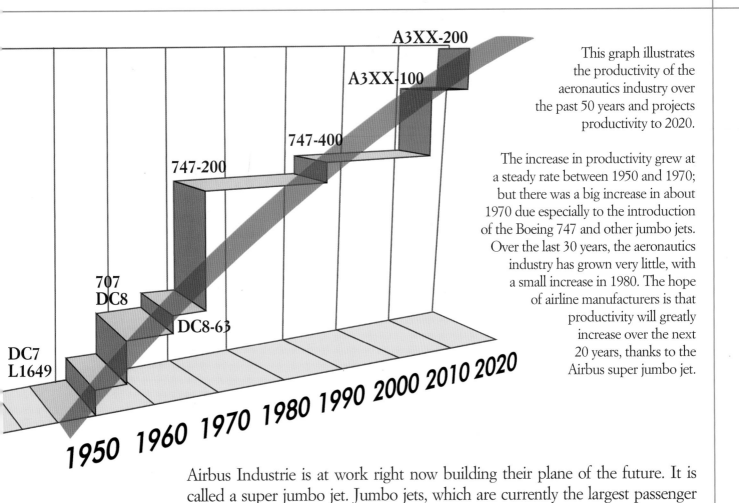

A3XX-200

A3XX-100

747-400

747-200

707
DC8

DC8-63

DC7
L1649

1950 1960 1970 1980 1990 2000 2010 2020

This graph illustrates the productivity of the aeronautics industry over the past 50 years and projects productivity to 2020.

The increase in productivity grew at a steady rate between 1950 and 1970; but there was a big increase in about 1970 due especially to the introduction of the Boeing 747 and other jumbo jets. Over the last 30 years, the aeronautics industry has grown very little, with a small increase in 1980. The hope of airline manufacturers is that productivity will greatly increase over the next 20 years, thanks to the Airbus super jumbo jet.

Airbus Industrie is at work right now building their plane of the future. It is called a super jumbo jet. Jumbo jets, which are currently the largest passenger planes, carry more than 400 passengers. Super jumbo jets are expected to carry up to 650 passengers. Airbus has named the super jumbo jet the A380. When the A380 takes to the sky, it will be the largest passenger plane ever built. Airbus plans to have the super jumbo ready for airline companies around 2005 or 2006. Many marvels of today's air travel were once thought to be impossible.

Below: This plane is being constructed in the Boeing factory.

This book will explore the science of aviation—in which things that seem impossible become reality. We will also look at the past, the present, and the future of aviation over the next five to ten years. Because of the competition between Airbus and Boeing, we will most likely see a whole new class of planes take to the sky. These planes will change air travel and aviation forever through size, shape, and speed.

Try, Try Again— Humans in Flight

Before exploring the present and the future of aviation, it is useful to know about aviation's past. Humans have wanted to master flight for thousands of years. Around 400 B.C., Archytas, a Greek scholar, built a flying bird. It was a wooden pigeon that circled in the air. No one really knows how he made his pigeon fly, but historians guess that he may have used steam to power the bird in some way.

The Chinese invented a flying model during the 300s B.C. It was the kite. In the 1500s A.D., inventor and artist Leonardo da Vinci made drawings of his version of humans flying. The drawings showed a person with human-made bird wings. It was proved in the 1600s that human muscles are too weak to flap human-made wings in order to fly. It wasn't until hundreds of years later that humans successfully took to the sky.

The first successful human flight was not in a plane, but in a hot-air balloon. A hot-air balloon is basically a large balloon with a basket attached to it. Pilots and passengers ride in the basket. The hot-air balloon can fly because it is filled with air that is lighter than the air in the sky. The sky has many different winds moving through it. A pilot finds these winds, which move the hot air balloon in various directions.

On November 21, 1783, two Frenchmen, named Doctor Jean Pilatre de Rozier and the Marquis d'Arlandes, were the first humans to fly in a hot-air balloon. The balloon, made by French brothers named Jacques and Joseph Montgolfier, remained in the air for a distance of more than 5 miles (8.04 km). It drifted over Paris for about 25 minutes.

Another advance in air travel was the invention of the glider. A glider is shaped like a kite, but unlike a kite, a glider is free to glide throughout the sky. Gliders are powered by the winds that blow through the sky. They are like airplanes that do not use engines.

Sir George Cayley built the first successful non-passenger glider in 1804. Later, he built the first successful passenger glider. Sir Cayley was born near Scarborough, England. He founded the science of aerodynamics. Aerodynamics is the study of objects in motion in the air. He is known as the father of modern aeronautics, or the science of aircraft.

Above: The balloon designed by Jacques and Joseph Montgolfier, illustrated above, was made of cloth and paper, and was first launched carrying animals in front of 130,000 spectators.

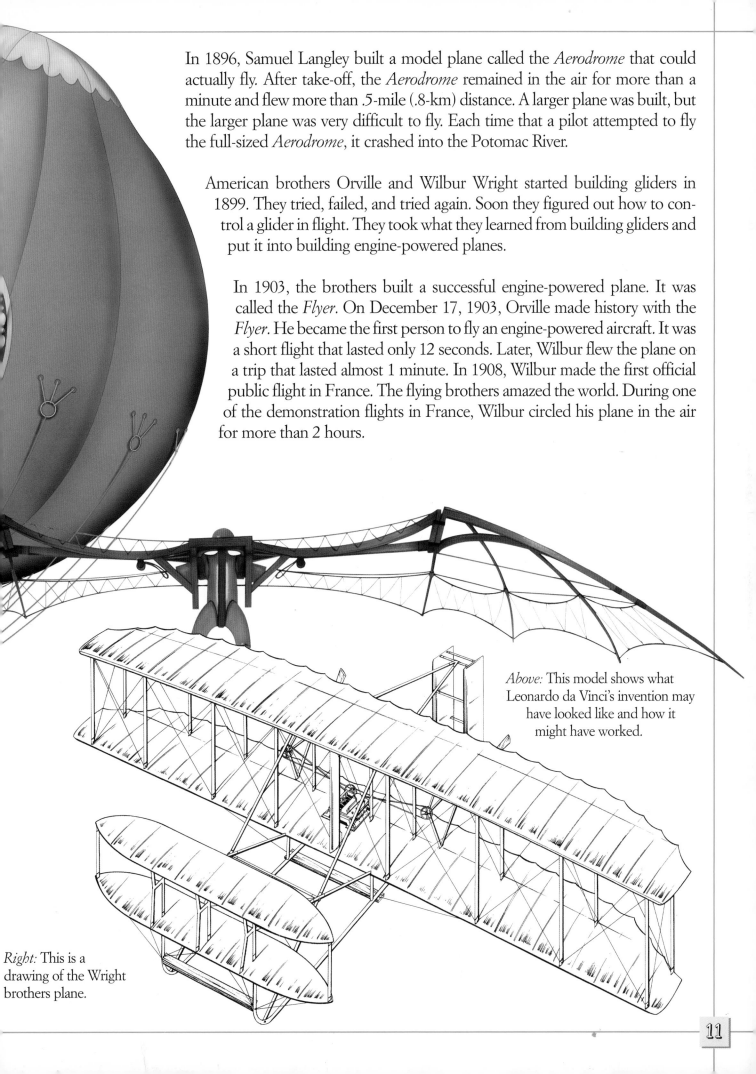

In 1896, Samuel Langley built a model plane called the *Aerodrome* that could actually fly. After take-off, the *Aerodrome* remained in the air for more than a minute and flew more than .5-mile (.8-km) distance. A larger plane was built, but the larger plane was very difficult to fly. Each time that a pilot attempted to fly the full-sized *Aerodrome*, it crashed into the Potomac River.

American brothers Orville and Wilbur Wright started building gliders in 1899. They tried, failed, and tried again. Soon they figured out how to control a glider in flight. They took what they learned from building gliders and put it into building engine-powered planes.

In 1903, the brothers built a successful engine-powered plane. It was called the *Flyer*. On December 17, 1903, Orville made history with the *Flyer*. He became the first person to fly an engine-powered aircraft. It was a short flight that lasted only 12 seconds. Later, Wilbur flew the plane on a trip that lasted almost 1 minute. In 1908, Wilbur made the first official public flight in France. The flying brothers amazed the world. During one of the demonstration flights in France, Wilbur circled his plane in the air for more than 2 hours.

Above: This model shows what Leonardo da Vinci's invention may have looked like and how it might have worked.

Right: This is a drawing of the Wright brothers plane.

Old Rivalry, New Planes

The largest and the fastest passenger plane is the Boeing 747. This jumbo jet can carry either 416 or 524 passengers, depending on the cabin's seating design. It flies at speeds of 565 miles per hour (910 km/h), at 35,000 feet (10,668 m) from the ground. The 747 is used all over the world by many airlines.

William Boeing founded the Boeing Company in 1927. The company introduced the 747 on September 30, 1968. Designing the largest and fastest passenger plane was a huge and an expensive project. Over 75,000 different engineering drawings were used to produce the first 747. Each 747, from the ground to its highest point, is as tall as a six-story building. From wing tip to tip, it is more than 200 feet (61 m) wide. Over forty cars could fit on the area of the wing.

A new factory was made that would allow the assembly of the enormous 747s. This huge factory—the size of forty football fields—cost Boeing $200 million to make. It would cost the company $1 billion to produce the jumbo 747. This project nearly put Boeing out of business, but soon airline companies started placing many orders for the plane. Boeing became the top jumbo plane builder in the world. Boeing has produced more than 15 versions of the 747 since 1970.

Other airline builders wanted to compete with Boeing. In 1972, British, French, German, and Spanish airplane builders formed a company called Airbus Industrie. Becoming one large company made competing with Boeing easier. The companies were able to share their resources and the costs of building and developing planes. This allowed Airbus to manufacture planes that could compete with the giant Boeing Company. Airbus built jumbos and many other types of passenger jet planes. Airline companies in the United States started to buy the Airbus jumbo planes in 1977.

Below: The only passenger plane that flies faster than the speed of sound is the Concorde. It flies at Mach 2, which is 1,350 miles (2,172 kilometers) per hour. It carries around 100 passengers.

The Concorde is extremely noisy. Because of its noise, the Concorde is not allowed to fly over the United States. If it makes a trip to the United States, it must land at a coastal airport.

The next step for Airbus was to offer something that Boeing did not. In 1994, Airbus decided to offer something bigger than the jumbo—the super jumbo. The Airbus super jumbo, or the A380 is expected to take its first test flight in 2004. Airline companies across the globe have already placed orders for the A380.

Right: The Sonic Cruiser has a very different design that will allow it to fly close to the speed of sound.

Below: British Airways has ordered the Airbus super jumbo.

Now Boeing has to come up with a better plane to keep their edge. At first Boeing said that it would make a super jumbo jet, too. Just recently however, Boeing decided that Airbus was making a mistake by building the super jumbo. Boeing believes that the super jumbo won't be the future of aviation. Instead, Boeing plans to introduce a new kind of passenger plane by 2007.

The latest designs from Boeing combine elements from both supersonic and jumbo jets to offer speed and size in one plane. This plane is not a super jumbo. It will, however, be a large passenger plane that travels just below the speed of sound. Boeing calls it the Sonic Cruiser.

The speed of sound is 760 miles per hour (1,225 km/h) here on Earth. As we move up and away from the Earth's surface, the speed of sound drops. Where jet planes fly, the speed of sound is around 660 miles per hour (1,062 km/h). This speed is also called Mach 1. The Sonic Cruiser would fly just below Mach 1. It is expected to fly at 648 miles per hour (1,042 km/h). Most passenger planes do not fly at this speed, because traveling at this speed can tear a regular plane apart. A special design is needed for a plane to travel safely at this speed.

If completed, the Sonic Cruiser will be the largest passenger plane flying just below Mach 1. The plane will seat from 200 to 300 people. Boeing is designing the plane so that it is not noisy like the Concorde. They believe that their plane will even take off and land more quietly than current planes. If the plane is successful, larger Sonic Cruisers also will be made.

The Concorde

Super jumbo jets are just one idea for commercial air travel. For many years now, the Concorde jet has been carrying passengers from one destination to another faster than the speed of sound. Supersonic airline research in Europe began in 1956 and resulted in the British and French governments signing an international treaty for the joint design, development, and manufacture of a supersonic airliner six years later. The first prototype was rolled out at Toulouse in 1967.

The Concorde measures 204 feet (62 m) in length but stretches as much as six to 10 inches (25.4 cm) while in flight due to heating of the frame. She is painted in a specially developed white paint to accommodate these changes and to dissipate the heat generated by supersonic flight. The wingspan is 83 feet 8 inches (25.5 m). This is much less than the wingspan of regular aircraft because Concorde flies in totally different way. The supersonic jet uses a special wing design called "Vortex Lift" to achieve her exceptional performance. Another special Concorde design feature is its nose. At take-off and landing, the nose is lowered to improve pilots' visibility.

The Concorde's four engines, specially designed Rolls-Royce/Snecma Olympus 593s, give more than 38,000 pounds of thrust each, with "reheat." Reheat adds fuel to the final stage of the engine to produce the extra power required for take-off and the transition to supersonic flight. They are the most powerful pure jet engines flying commercially. Using these powerful engines, the Concorde takes off at 220 knots (250 mph) (compared with 165 knots for most subsonic aircraft). It cruises at around 1,350 mph (2,172.6 km/h), which is more than twice the speed of sound! The Concorde also flies at a different altitude than do most jets, reaching an altitude of up to 60,000 feet (18.3 km). That's over 11 miles high. A typical London to New York crossing takes a little less than three and a half hours as opposed to about eight hours for a subsonic flight. Traveling westward, the five-hour time difference means the Concorde effectively arrives before she has taken off. That's fast!

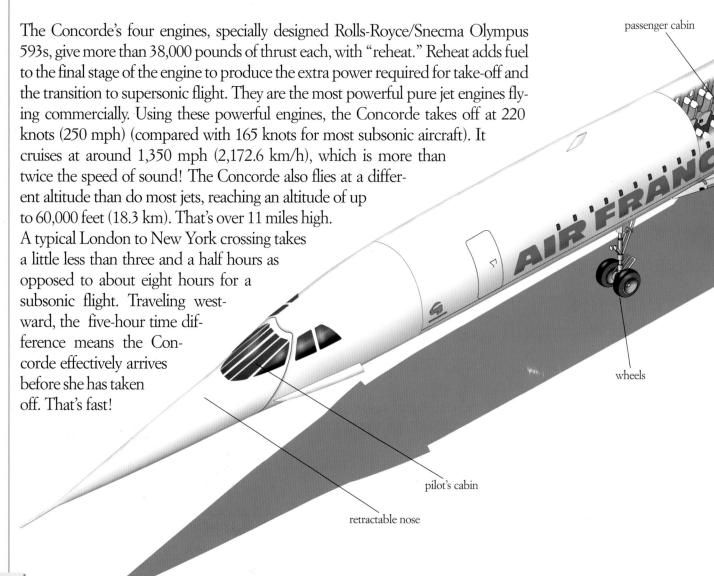

passenger cabin

wheels

pilot's cabin

retractable nose

Despite the benefits of traveling at such high speeds, there are drawbacks to the Concorde, such as noise pollution and fuel inefficiency, that have pushed airlines to continue searching for better ways to carry passengers. One of these ways was to build a super jumbo. A super jumbo can carry more people, is less expensive to operate, and is far less damaging to the environment. Super jumbos are just one more step in trying to improve air travel for customers.

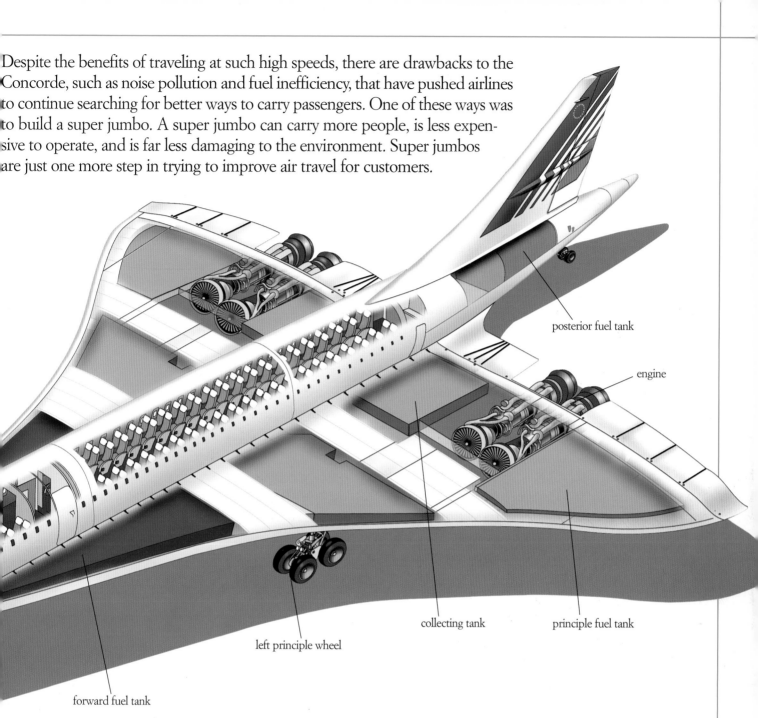

posterior fuel tank

engine

collecting tank

principle fuel tank

left principle wheel

forward fuel tank

THE TRANSFERRING OF FUEL DURING THE VARIOUS PHASES OF FLIGHT

The yellow arrows in each drawing show how the fuel is shifted in each phase of the flight. This is done to shift the weight in the plane so that it remains balanced.

1) intermediate acceleration phase
2) the end of passage into supersonic phase
3) landing phase

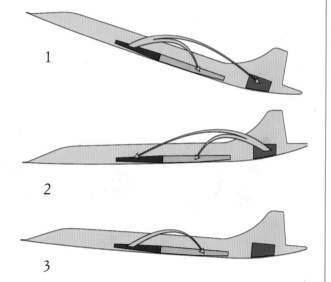

1

2

3

Forces of Flight

Sir George Cayley's study of aircraft and aerodynamics allowed people to see how objects fly, and how they can remain in flight. Cayley and other aviation enthusiasts found that there are several aspects to flying.

When an object moves through the air, several forces, or energies, work for and against that object. Scientists study these forces in order to understand flight. By studying the forces, we can learn how to make flying easier and more successful. We can also learn how to avoid crashes and flight failures.

There are four main forces that allow a plane to fly. They are gravity, lift, drag, and thrust. A careful balance of these four forces will allow a plane to fly. When the forces are out of balance, a plane is more likely to crash, or fly improperly.

Gravity is a strong, natural force of Earth. It is what keeps us on the Earth's surface. We can jump and can leave the ground for a second, but gravity pulls us right back down. Gravity pulls on a plane while it's in flight. In order to fly, another force is needed to work against gravity. That force is called lift.

Lift is a force that is created by the plane's wing and motion. Lift pushes a plane upward, away from the ground. It's a force that is created as the plane's wing moves through the air. The faster a plane moves, the more lift that the wing creates. Eventually, the lift becomes strong enough to lift the plane off the ground.

Without moving forward, a plane cannot create lift. Without lift, the plane will not fly. What allows the plane to move forward is called thrust. Thrust is a force that is created by engines that are attached to the plane. Engines move the plane forward at speeds that will be fast enough to create lift.

Drag is a natural force of air. Drag pushes against a plane while it's moving forward. Drag works against the thrust of an airplane. If the amount of drag is reduced, the plane will take flight. In order to reduce the amount of drag, planes are made in smooth, sleek designs. Engines are also made with enough power to work against drag. In order for flight to occur, there must be lift working against gravity and thrust working against drag.

In order to bring a plane back to Earth, the balance of the forces must be changed. The engine power, which creates thrust, must be decreased. As the engines slow, so does the plane. This decreases thrust, as well as lift. Slowing the engines allows the plane to come back down, or to descend to Earth.

Right: This diagram shows the four different forces of flight. Thrust is the forward motion caused by the plane's engines. Weight is the force of gravity acting against the heavy plane and trying to pull it down. Lift is the force that allows the plane to take off and to remain in the sky. Finally, drag is the force of the air as it passes around the plane.

Right: This diagram shows how lift works. This is called the Bernoulli Effect. Because of the special shape of the wing, air travels more quickly over the top, which creates a low pressure area. The air traveling beneath the wing has greater pressure so it pushes the wing up, or lifts it.

Right: These drawings show various high-lift devices used on jet-powered planes such as jumbo jets and super jumbo jets. They are used in landing and in taking off to increase or to decrease the amount of lift. The red shapes show how these devices, called flaps, move during take-off and landing in order to increase lift. Notice some wings have a single flap, while others have two or even three flaps.

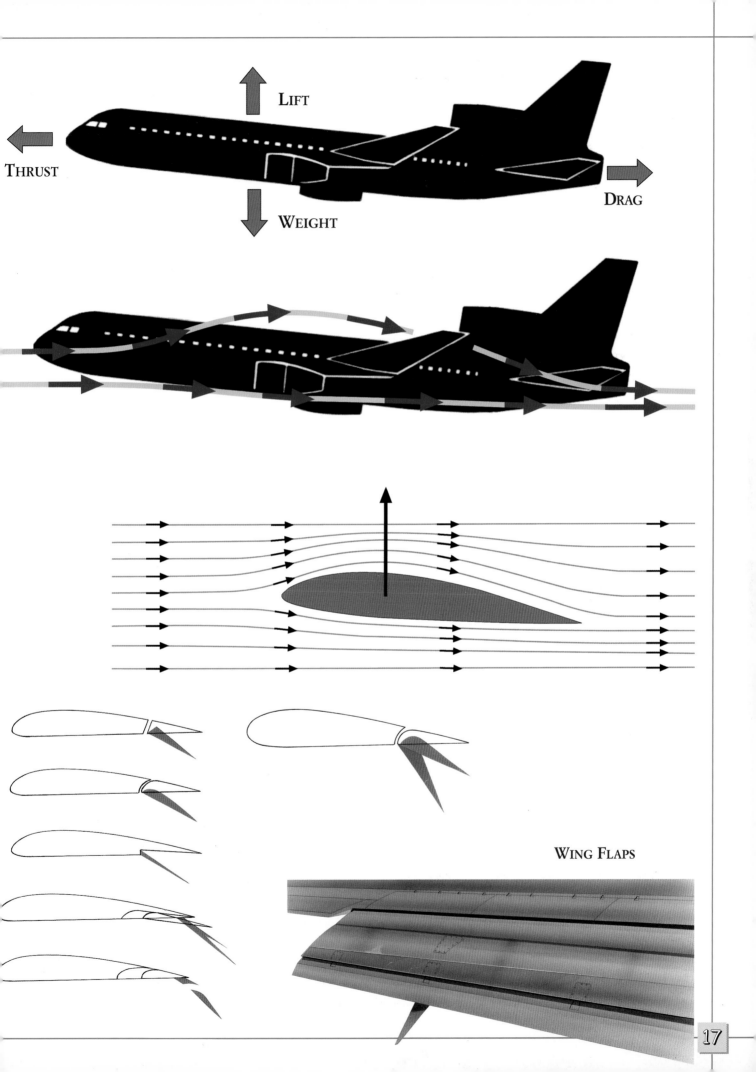

LIFT

THRUST

WEIGHT

DRAG

WING FLAPS

The Airbus A380

Today's largest passenger plane, the 747, has a price tag of $183 million. The cost of each A380, the first super jumbo jet, will be $240 million. Airbus estimates that it will cost more than $12 billion to design and to produce the A380. Airbus feels that having the largest passenger plane in the sky makes the huge investment worthwhile. To ensure the success of the A380, other versions of the plane also will be offered.

As with the A380, all other versions are planned to be more environmentally friendly than airplanes flying today. Older planes were built when the environment was not a priority. They burn a lot of fuel, which can damage our environment. The older planes are also very loud. New planes, such as the A380 will be designed to use less fuel. The A380 family will also make less noise while flying than do current large passenger planes.

The standard A380 passenger model will be delivered to clients in 2006. Another version of the plane will be offered in 2006 as well. It will be the A380 freight model. This plane will carry freight or cargo, rather than carrying people.

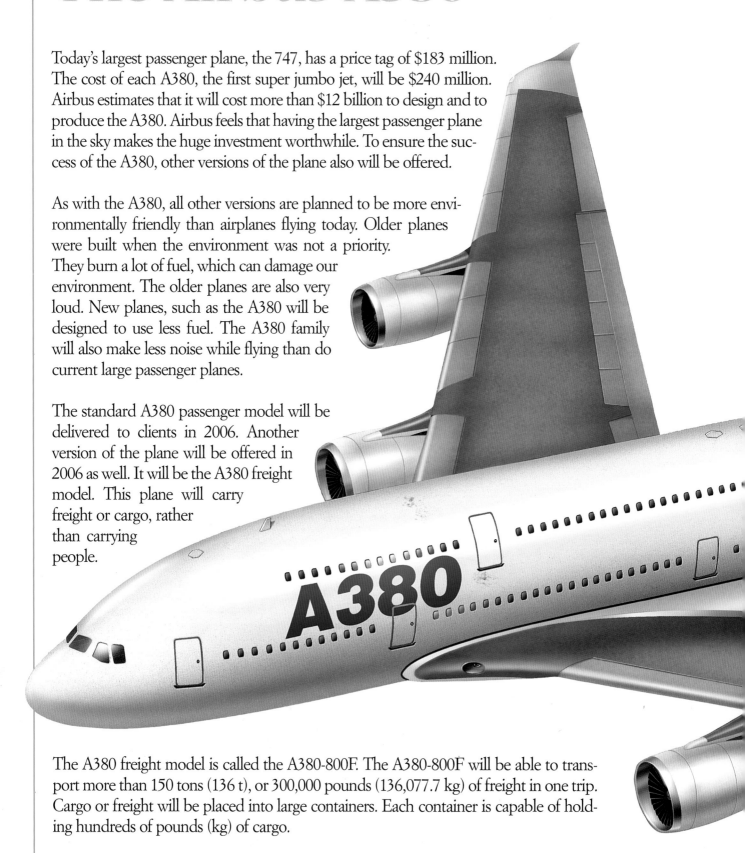

The A380 freight model is called the A380-800F. The A380-800F will be able to transport more than 150 tons (136 t), or 300,000 pounds (136,077.7 kg) of freight in one trip. Cargo or freight will be placed into large containers. Each container is capable of holding hundreds of pounds (kg) of cargo.

The A380-880F will fly more than 5,000 miles (8,046.7 km) in one trip. By using the freight super jumbo, delivery and airline companies can ship tons (t) of freight in one trip. This will save the companies money and time.

Airbus isn't stopping at just adding a freight model. According to Aerospaceweb.org, there will be even more models of the A380 offered over the next five to ten years. Aerospaceweb.org is an organization of aviation engineers that provides aviation information as well as an online aircraft museum for the public.

A380 DETAILS
WING SPAN: 261 feet, 10 inches (79.8 m)
LENGTH: 239 feet, 6 inches (73 m)
HEIGHT: 79 feet, 1 inch (24.1 m)
PASSENGERS: 555
CRUISING SPEED: 630 mph (1,013 km)
FLIGHT ALTITUDE: 43,000 feet (13,106 m)
CARGO: 12 cargo containers
DISTANCE: 8,150 miles (15,100 km)
ENGINES: 4 Trent 900 turbofans/
4 GP 7200 turbofans

A380-800F DETAILS
WING SPAN: 261 feet, 10 inches (79.8 m)
LENGTH: 239 feet, 6 inches (73.0 m)
HEIGHT: 79 feet, 1 inch (24.1 m)
PASSENGERS: None
UPPER DECK: 17 cargo containers
MAIN DECK: 28 cargo containers
LOWER DECK: 12 cargo containers
DISTANCE: 5,650 miles (10,410 kilometers)
CARGO/FREIGHT WEIGHT: 150 tons (136 t),
     or 331,000 pounds (150,139 kg).

Jet Engines— Masters of Thrust

Without thrust, heavy planes such as the 747 and A380 couldn't fly. One of the most effective engines that creates thrust is the jet engine. Sir Frank Whittle invented the jet engine. In 1928, Whittle began a long process of designing and building the jet engine.

In 1939, Whittle finally created a good design. His design proved that jet power was possible. A plane called the Gloster E28/39 was built with the new jet engine. On May 15, 1941, the Gloster E28/39 took flight. As the jet plane streaked through the sky, amazed onlookers saw the future of aviation. Today, all planes except small planes are powered by jet engines.

Today's jet engines make it possible for planes weighing thousands of pounds to lift off the ground. They make it possible to break the sound barrier, or the speed of sound. Jet engines also allow planes to fly at high altitudes. Altitude is a measurement of how high an object is in the sky.

High altitudes are 35,000 feet (10,668 m) or higher from Earth's surface. Planes flying at lower altitudes are affected by more weather conditions, such as clouds and winds. When planes fly through these conditions, the planes experience turbulence. Turbulence makes the flight bumpy. By flying at higher altitudes, a plane can avoid turbulence, which makes for a smoother flight.

Jet engines use air, fuel, flames, and electricity to move an object forward, or to create thrust. Powerful gases are released from the back of jet engines, which causes the engine and the plane to thrust forward. There are four types of jet engines. They are the turbojet, the turboprop, the ramjet, and the turbofan. All four types create thrust in basically the same way.

Air gets sucked into the engine. The air is squeezed into a tight space, which increases the air's pressure. The air is then forced into a special chamber. In the chamber, the air is mixed with fuel. The mixture is set on fire, which creates powerful gases. The gases blast toward the back of the engine with great force. As the gases escape from the back of the engine, the engine moves, or thrusts forward. Jet engines are housed in nacelles. Nacelles are casings that allow the jet engine to be attached to the plane.

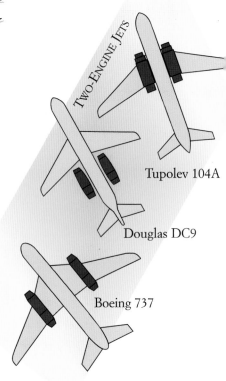

TWO-ENGINE JETS

Tupolev 104A

Douglas DC9

Boeing 737

Right, middle: To understand how thrust is created, imagine how you would blow up a balloon. As you fill a balloon with air, the air gets squeezed into a tight space. The force of the squeezed air begins to push outward, which makes the balloon grow larger. Because the air inside the balloon is squeezed, it has force, or power. If you let go of the balloon, the escaping air sends the balloon zinging about the room.

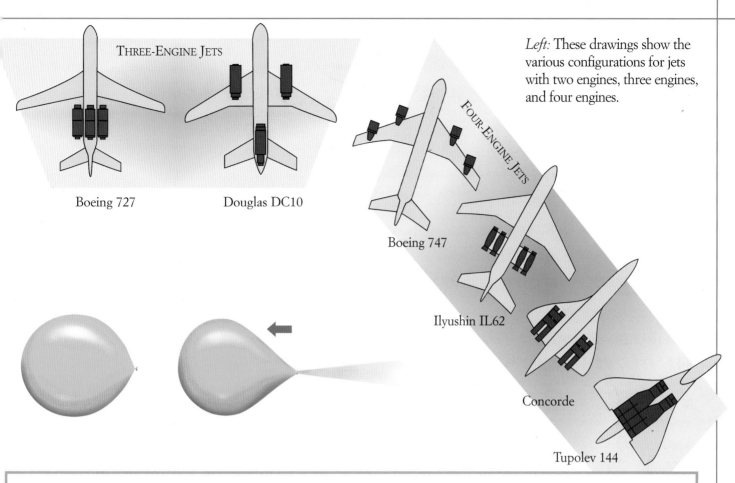

THREE-ENGINE JETS

Boeing 727

Douglas DC10

Left: These drawings show the various configurations for jets with two engines, three engines, and four engines.

FOUR-ENGINE JETS

Boeing 747

Ilyushin IL62

Concorde

Tupolev 144

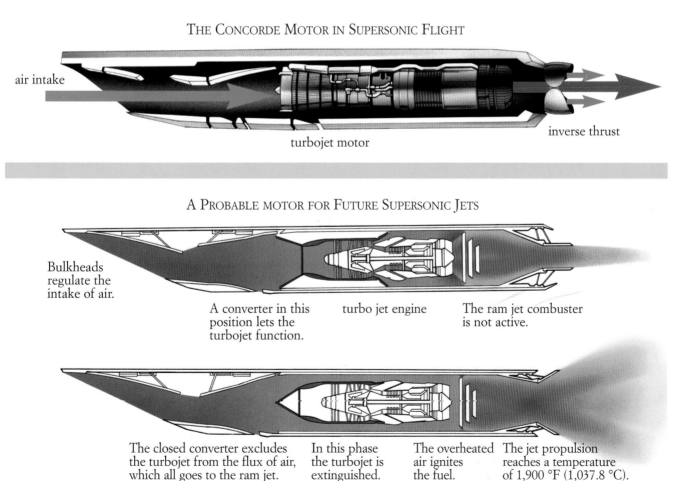

THE CONCORDE MOTOR IN SUPERSONIC FLIGHT

air intake

turbojet motor

inverse thrust

A PROBABLE MOTOR FOR FUTURE SUPERSONIC JETS

Bulkheads regulate the intake of air.

A converter in this position lets the turbojet function.

turbo jet engine

The ram jet combuster is not active.

The closed converter excludes the turbojet from the flux of air, which all goes to the ram jet.

In this phase the turbojet is extinguished.

The overheated air ignites the fuel.

The jet propulsion reaches a temperature of 1,900 °F (1,037.8 °C).

The Turbofan Power

Various engine builders make jet engines. These builders are also called aero-engine builders. The two major aero-engine builders are Rolls-Royce and the Engine Alliance. Rolls-Royce has branches in more than 48 countries, but the company began in England. The Engine Alliance is American. Both companies sell their engines to airline companies and to airplane builders all over the world. Airbus has asked both Rolls-Royce and the Engine Alliance to design a turbofan engine for the A380. Airline companies who buy the super jumbo will be able to choose either company's engine.

The power of a jet engine can be measured by the amount of its thrust. Thrust is measured in pounds. One pound of thrust will be able to keep a 1 pound (.45 kg) object in the air. Three thousand pounds of thrust will be able to keep a 3,000 pound (1,360.8 kg) object in the air. The more thrust an engine can produce, the more weight it can lift off the ground. For super jumbo jets to be successful, there must be engines powerful enough to lift them off the ground.

Engineers design engines that can produce several thousand pounds (kg) of thrust. The problem is that these engines can become very heavy. Researchers try to find lighter metals and materials. Lighter materials also keep the engine and the plane light. The materials must be strong enough to withstand the power and heat of a jet engine.

Various parts of a jet engine can create temperatures as high as 2,800 °F (1,537 °C). Constant exposure to this temperature can melt and damage many materials. Engine parts are made with various materials including metal. Engineers can combine various metals and materials to make stronger, more powerful substances for use in engines. Materials include metals such as nickel, titanium, aluminum, and other materials such as plastics and ceramics.

Turbofans are designed to give the most thrust, without making the engine too heavy. Turbofans use air in two ways to create thrust. Air goes inside the engine, as with most other jet engines, to

Right: This is a cutaway of a turbofan engine.

Below: Closeup of a jet engine at the Boeing factory.

Bottom left: The GP7200 is Engine Alliance's turbofan.

GP 7200

create thrust. Air is also sent along the outside of the engine, and toward the back.

This air gets used to create more thrust at the back of the engine. This flow of air over the outside of the engine also quiets the noise made by the engine. This makes the turbofan less noisy than the other jet engines.

Looking Inside a Turbofan

The main parts of a turbofan jet engine from the front of the engine to the back, are the fan, the compressor, the combustion chamber, the turbine, and the nozzle. Most parts are coated in special materials, including iron, nickel, copper, titanium, and cement, to help them withstand the extreme heat and pressure they undergo with each use.

Right: This is a diagram of the influx of gas turbine engine LM2500. This type of General Electric turbine, derives from civil and military airplanes, (such as the Boeing 747), and is largely used for marine vessels.

The **turbine** is used to help power the fan, and the compressor. As high-pressure gases blast from the combustion chamber, they pass through the turbine. The turbine recycles some of the energy from the force of the gases rushing through it. This energy is used to turn the fan and to power the compressor. The turbine is usually made from nickel. The turbine is coated with special materials, such as iron, nickel, copper, cement, and ceramics, that help the turbine withstand extreme heat from the high-pressure gases.

The **combustion chamber** is where the compressed air is forced to enter. The air is mixed with fuel and then burned. Burning the air and fuel mixture creates high-pressure gases. The combustion chamber is usually made from nickel.

The **fan** sucks a great amount of air into and over the engine. The fan is usually made from titanium. Titanium is a lightweight metal.

The **compressor** squeezes the air that enters the engine. Air packed into a tight space increases the air's pressure. The parts of the compressor are usually made from nickel and titanium. Both are light metals.

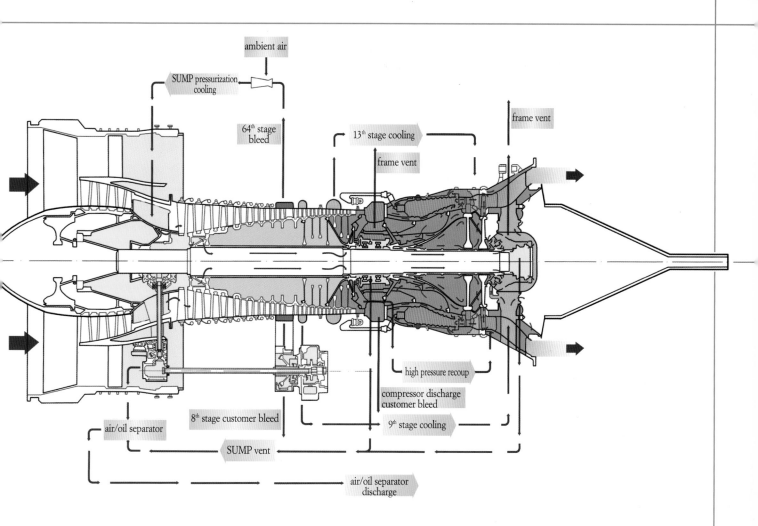

ambient air

SUMP pressurization cooling

64th stage bleed

13th stage cooling

frame vent

frame vent

high pressure recoup

compressor discharge customer bleed

8th stage customer bleed

9th stage cooling

air/oil separator

SUMP vent

air/oil separator discharge

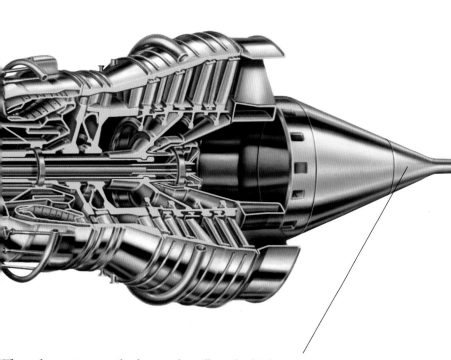

The **exhaust** is a nozzle designed to allow the high-pressure gases to leave the engine. Gases pass through the nozzle at speeds of more than 1,000 miles per hour (1,609 km/h). The force of the gases exiting the engine creates thrust. Turbofan nozzles are made from nickel, titanium and ceramic-based substances.

Some turbofan engines also use an afterburner. The afterburner is a second combustion chamber. It is located between the turbine and the nozzle. Afterburners create additional thrust, but they also use a lot of fuel. Afterburners are used very sparingly. Pilots can use afterburners for added thrust during take off or in emergencies.

Rolls-Royce and the Engine Alliance are in the process of building and testing their turbofan designs for the super jumbo jet, the A380. Rolls-Royce has named their engine the Trent 900. The Engine Alliance has named their engine the GP7200.

The Airbus Cutaway

There are many parts to an airplane that all contribute to its ability to fly, its safety in the air, and customer comfort. This labeled diagram shows all the parts that make up an Airbus jumbo jet.

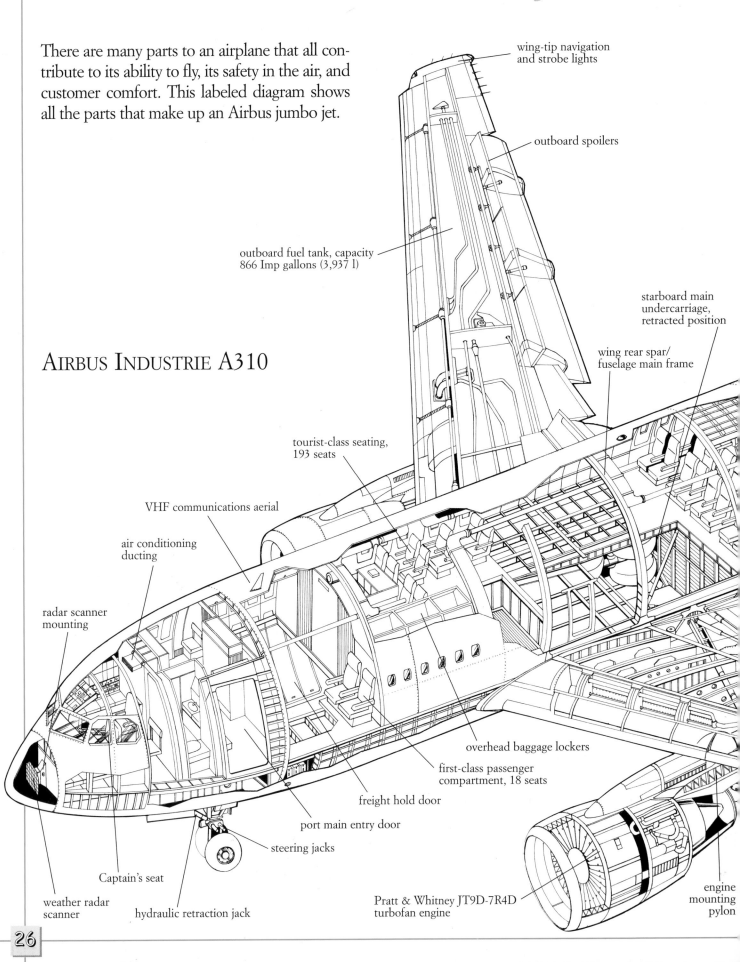

AIRBUS INDUSTRIE A310

wing-tip navigation and strobe lights

outboard spoilers

outboard fuel tank, capacity 866 Imp gallons (3,937 l)

starboard main undercarriage, retracted position

wing rear spar/ fuselage main frame

tourist-class seating, 193 seats

VHF communications aerial

air conditioning ducting

radar scanner mounting

overhead baggage lockers

first-class passenger compartment, 18 seats

freight hold door

port main entry door

steering jacks

Captain's seat

weather radar scanner

hydraulic retraction jack

Pratt & Whitney JT9D-7R4D turbofan engine

engine mounting pylon

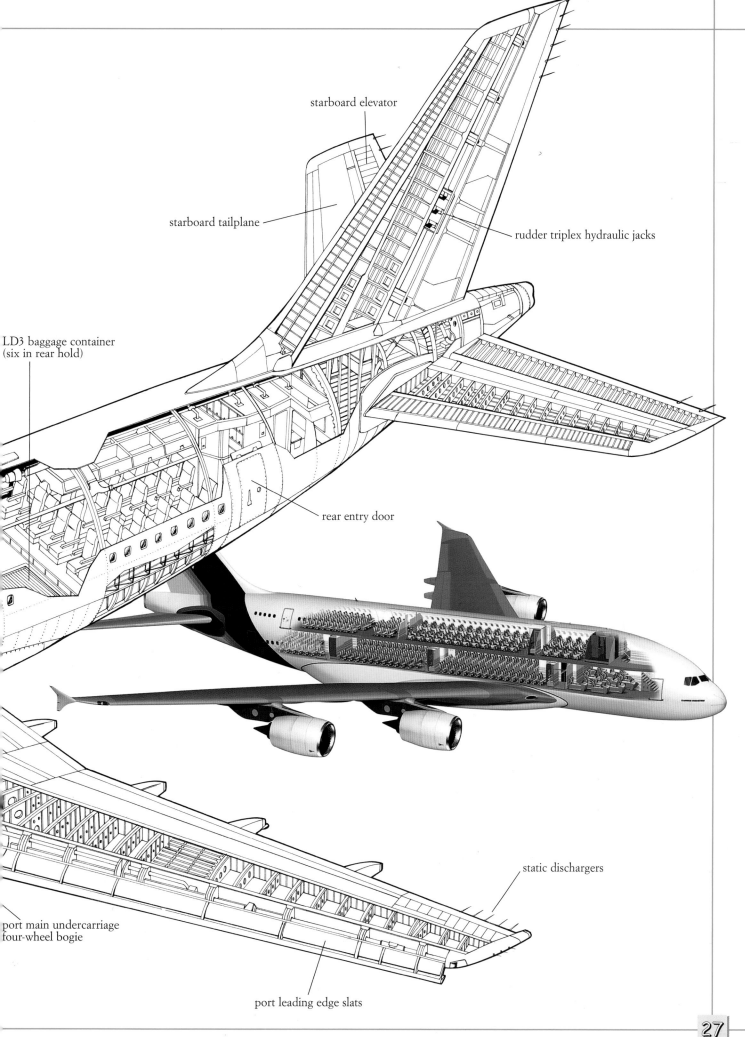

starboard elevator

starboard tailplane

rudder triplex hydraulic jacks

LD3 baggage container
(six in rear hold)

rear entry door

static dischargers

port main undercarriage
four-wheel bogie

port leading edge slats

The Jumbo Generation

One of the most competitive jets of the last generation was the Lockheed tri-jet N1011 (TriStar). Created in the same days as its direct competitor, the McDonnell Douglas (now partnered with Boeing) DC 10, TriStar had to compete also with Boeing's larger, four-engine 747 jumbo jet and the emerging Airbus twin, the A300B2. The technology, such as new lightweight materials and super-powerful yet fuel-efficient engines, used to create these larger wide-body jets starting in the 1970s has paved the way for airplane manufacturers to think about building even bigger aircraft and to make smaller aircraft work even more efficiently.

In their early versions, the slightly larger DC 10 with its General Electric CF6-6 turbo-fans and the TriStar with its Rolls-Royce RB211 turbofans, achieved similar take-off power. With twice as much thrust, their engines showed significant advances in performance over earlier jet engines. The engines allowed the heavier jets to get more lift and to fly farther with less fuel.

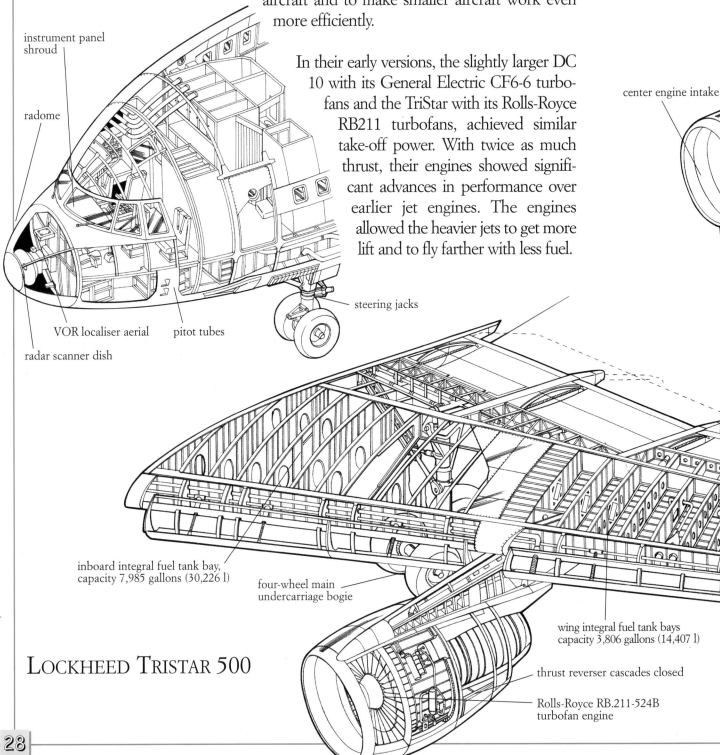

instrument panel shroud

radome

center engine intake

VOR localiser aerial

pitot tubes

steering jacks

radar scanner dish

inboard integral fuel tank bay, capacity 7,985 gallons (30,226 l)

four-wheel main undercarriage bogie

wing integral fuel tank bays capacity 3,806 gallons (14,407 l)

thrust reverser cascades closed

Rolls-Royce RB.211-524B turbofan engine

LOCKHEED TRISTAR 500

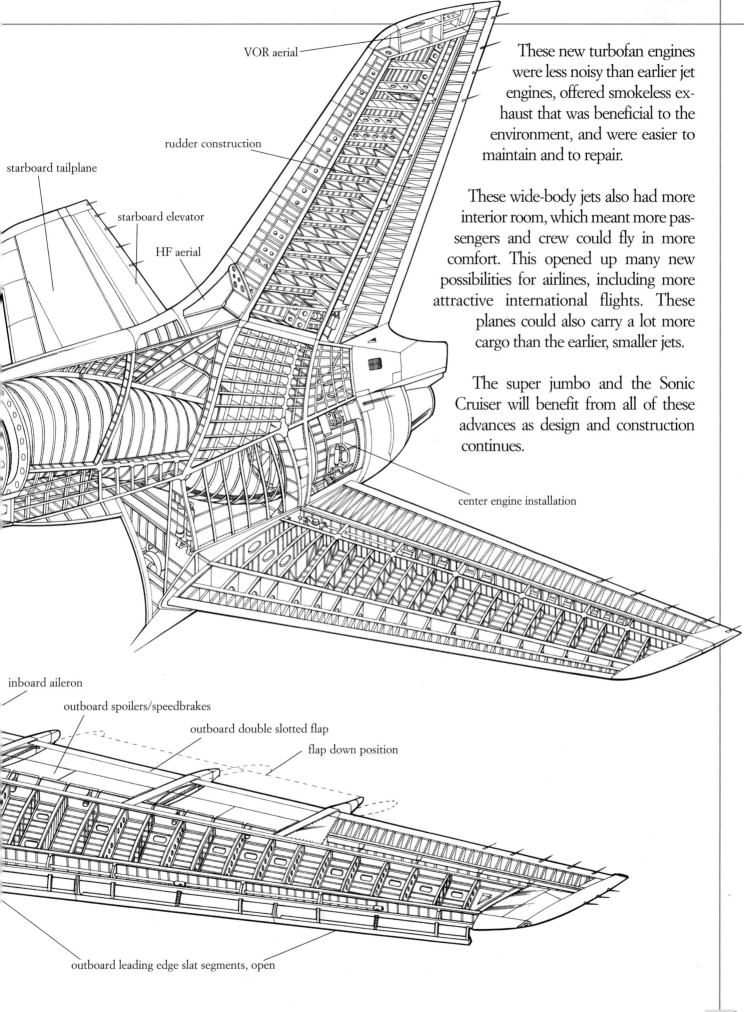

VOR aerial

rudder construction

starboard tailplane

starboard elevator

HF aerial

These new turbofan engines were less noisy than earlier jet engines, offered smokeless exhaust that was beneficial to the environment, and were easier to maintain and to repair.

These wide-body jets also had more interior room, which meant more passengers and crew could fly in more comfort. This opened up many new possibilities for airlines, including more attractive international flights. These planes could also carry a lot more cargo than the earlier, smaller jets.

The super jumbo and the Sonic Cruiser will benefit from all of these advances as design and construction continues.

center engine installation

inboard aileron

outboard spoilers/speedbrakes

outboard double slotted flap

flap down position

outboard leading edge slat segments, open

An International Project

The Airbus super jumbo jet is not built in one huge building. Sections of the plane are assembled at different company sites all over Europe. Plane sections are assembled and then flown to the next site. Airbus built a special plane that is large enough to transport other plane parts. It is the Super Transporter A300-600ST. Smaller parts of the A380 will be transported using the A300-600ST. The individually assembled sections, however, are too large for the Super Transporter. Super jumbo sections will be transported by boats and by ground vehicles. A completed A380 is enormous at about 239 feet (73 m) in length. Its wing span is even bigger, almost 262 feet (79.8 m).

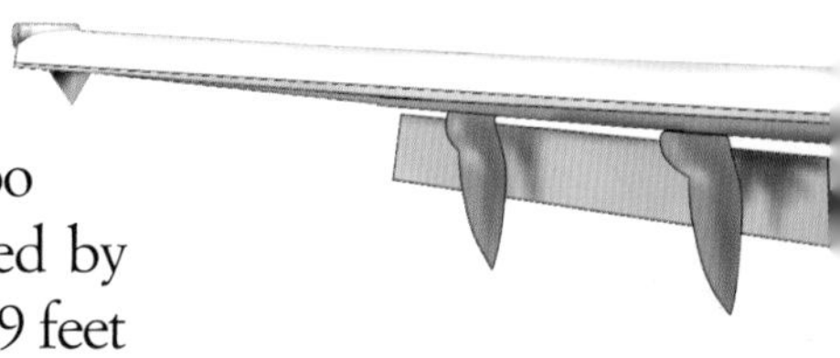

Below: Both these drawings give information about where different parts of the plane are built and then assembled.

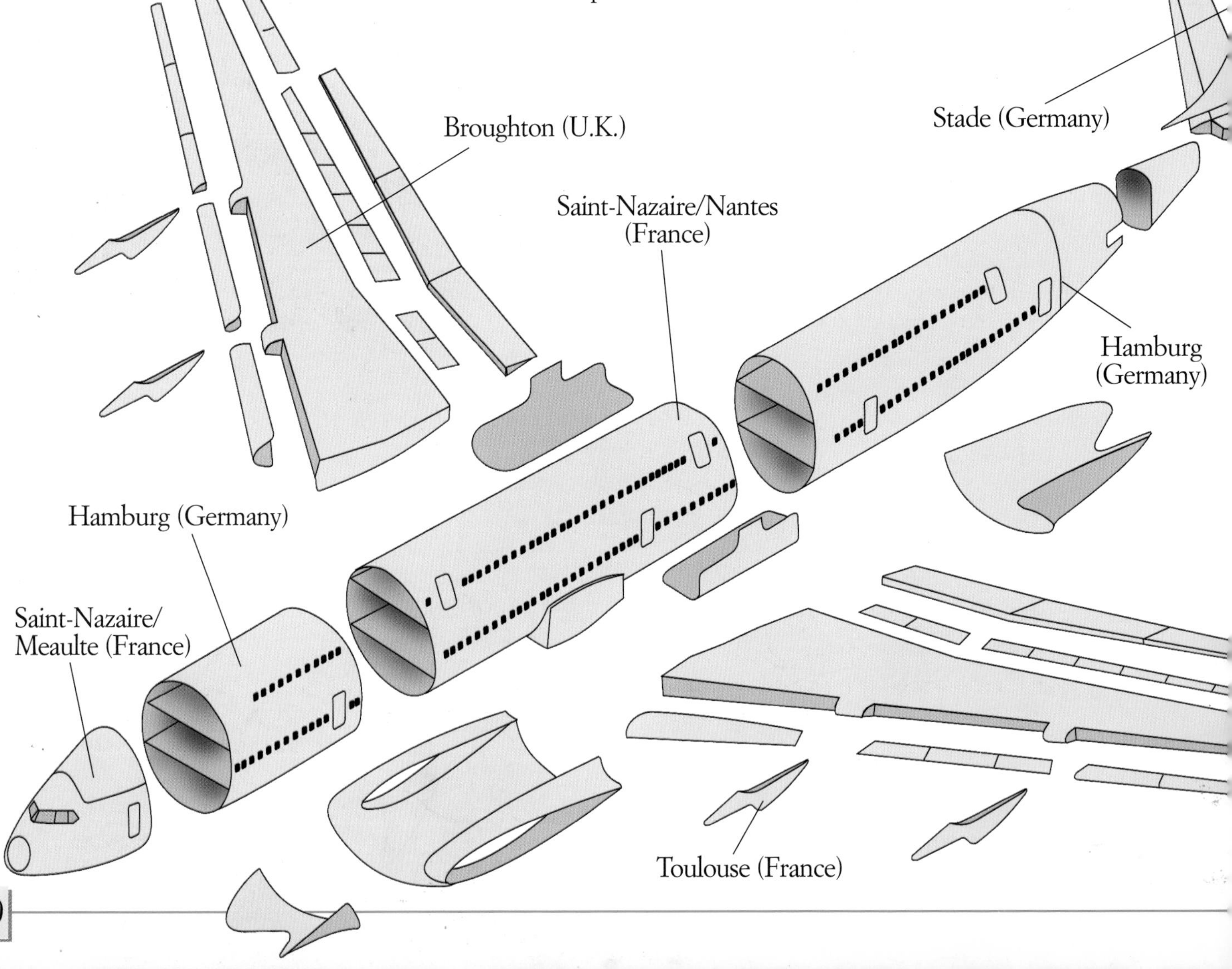

Broughton (U.K.)

Saint-Nazaire/Nantes (France)

Stade (Germany)

Hamburg (Germany)

Hamburg (Germany)

Saint-Nazaire/ Meaulte (France)

Toulouse (France)

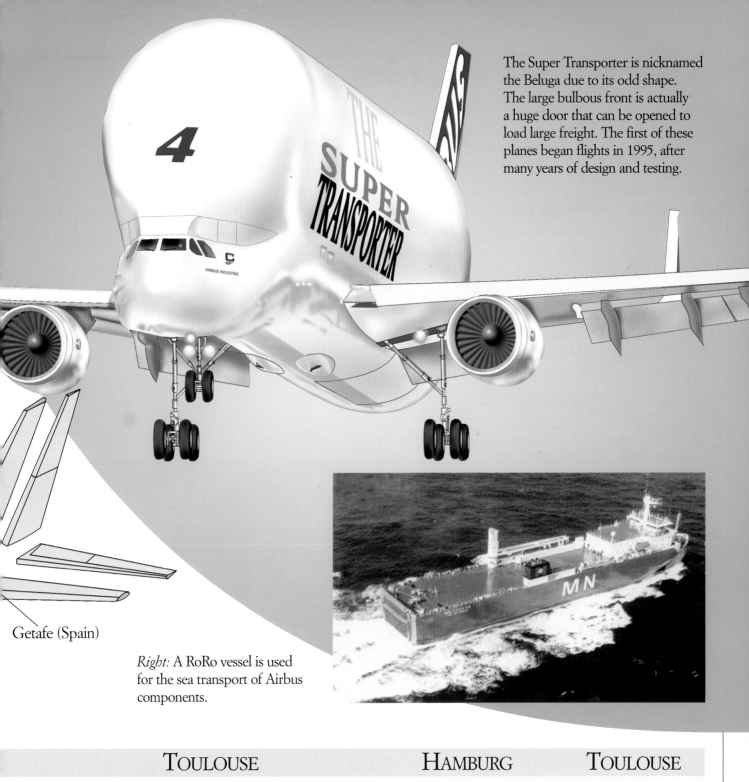

The Super Transporter is nicknamed the Beluga due to its odd shape. The large bulbous front is actually a huge door that can be opened to load large freight. The first of these planes began flights in 1995, after many years of design and testing.

Getafe (Spain)

Right: A RoRo vessel is used for the sea transport of Airbus components.

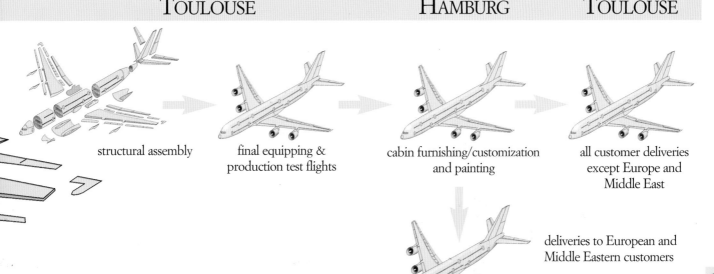

TOULOUSE	HAMBURG	TOULOUSE

structural assembly

final equipping & production test flights

cabin furnishing/customization and painting

all customer deliveries except Europe and Middle East

deliveries to European and Middle Eastern customers

Construction

After each piece of the super jumbo jet is completed, the sections will be sent to Toulouse, France. This is where all of the pieces will be assembled together to form the main structure. The engines will also be installed, making the plane able to fly. Then it will be flown to Hamburg, Germany. There, the cabin, and various systems will be installed, painted, and finished. Airbus expects that the planes will be flying by 2005 or early 2006.

The fuselage will be high-tech and light. The fuselage is the plane's body. The outer shell of the fuselage will be made with a new material made from glass fiber and aluminum. This material will be light, durable, and fire resistant. Airbus estimates that the new materials used for the outer shell will save 3 tons (2.7 t) of weight.

Systems such as the landing gear will be designed to deliver the super jumbo safely to the ground. There will be twenty landing gear wheels under the A380. Airbus says that each wheel will have less weight on it than a wheel under a 747.

Below: A section of the body of the plane is being constructed in the factory.

In the construction of the super jumbo, laser beams will be used to weld and to attach parts together. Currently, parts are fastened together using rivets, or nails. Laser beams will reduce the amount of time that it takes to assemble a plane. It will also reduce the weight and the cost of the super jumbo. Laser welded parts are also believed to last longer than rivet fastened parts.

Airbus plans to use the newest high-tech materials for the super jumbo. They will use these special materials to make the plane strong, safe, and light. New materials include carbon fiber and metallic compounds, or mixtures of different metals. Forty percent of the A380 will be made of the most advanced metallic materials known to humans.

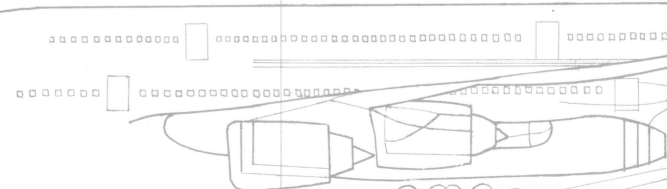

Above: Jumbo jets and super jumbos are constructed in pieces, which then need to be attached together either by riveting or welding. Above are images of the cabin section of the plane in various stages of construction.

Super Jumbo Design

During the design process, Airbus asked several people from the aviation community for design suggestions. Representatives from fifty airports and twenty airline companies were asked to help in the development of the A380 design. Airbus also asked about 1,200 frequent fliers for their suggestions on the cabin design.

Looking at a piece of a jumbo jet or super jumbo jet skeleton, it might seem like the design is pretty simple. In some ways this is true. But in order to make that simple rounded body there are many things that must be taken into account by designers. The walls must be strong yet flexible, to resist wind forces, heat, and cold. They must be as thin and as light as possible and still be structurally sound. There are many things such as these that must be taken into account as the plane is constructed.

There are reinforcing bars in the plane body and wings called ribs and spars that provide strength but must also be flexible. Wings must be designed with wing flaps and other devices to help provide lift and to increase or decrease drag depending on what the plane is doing.

For things like windows and doors special care must be paid to design. A door must be able to close in such a way that the plane becomes completely airtight. If they did not work properly the plane could be torn apart, or at the very least it would become very uncomfortable for passengers as the air pressure changed. Windows must be made of special material that can withstand extreme temperatures. So, the jumbo jet and super jumbo jet design may look simple, but remember you can't judge a plane by its skeleton!

Above and right: The body of an Airbus plane is being constructed in a large factory. Note that the shell, or exoskeleton of the plane is relatively thin. High-tech materials are used to construct a light-weight, durable plane body.

Above: A Boeing machinist is checking newly-made pieces of a plane's skeleton. The pieces were made with extremely fast and precise metal-cutting machinery.

High-Tech Materials

In order to make a super jumbo jet operate safely and efficiently, some new advanced materials will be used in the design and the construction of the planes. Some of these materials have been chosen because they will require very little maintenance for the airplane to continue to run in top form. Glare is one such material. It is a laminate made from alternating layers of aluminum and glass-fiber reinforced adhesive. Glare is 10 percent less dense than aluminum and lasts much longer. The material is very resistant to corrosion because of the glass layer, and it is quite easy to repair.

Another innovation used on the super jumbo is a fuselage shell that is laserwelded, rather than fastened by bolts. This will make the structure more durable and lighter in weight. It also saves a lot of construction time over riveting, because it is one smooth and continuous process. Another benefit is the elimination of holes. Every time a rivet is placed, it creates a hole in the fuselage. These holes are very susceptible to corrosion and to cracking over time. Welding avoids this problem.

The super jumbo fin and tail-plane, as well as the rear pressure bulkhead and fuselage center section, will all be constructed with carbon-fiber reinforced plastics (CFRP). The main wing structure will be made from conventional as well as advanced metallic composites.

Another exciting new material is being used on the super jumbo that will also increase its durability. It is called Super Plastic Forming, Diffusing Bonded (SPFDB) titanium. It is used on the parts of the plane that undergo large stresses or high temperatures. The SPFDB titanium has a more rigid, strong structure than normal titanium.

All of these advanced materials and technologies are what make it possible to make ever bigger and faster airplanes. Jets built using older technologies simply could not stand up to all the added weight and pressure of a larger or faster plane. Who knows what the next twenty years might bring in the way of exciting new technologies. Each new advance opens the door for new designs that were never before posible!

Right: The new Airbus super jumbo is constructed from new, high-tech materials.

Below: All parts of the aircraft must be tested to make sure they can withstand the maximum amount of pressure they might face during operation. A high-pressure hydraulic test bench, like this one, is used to test the pieces.

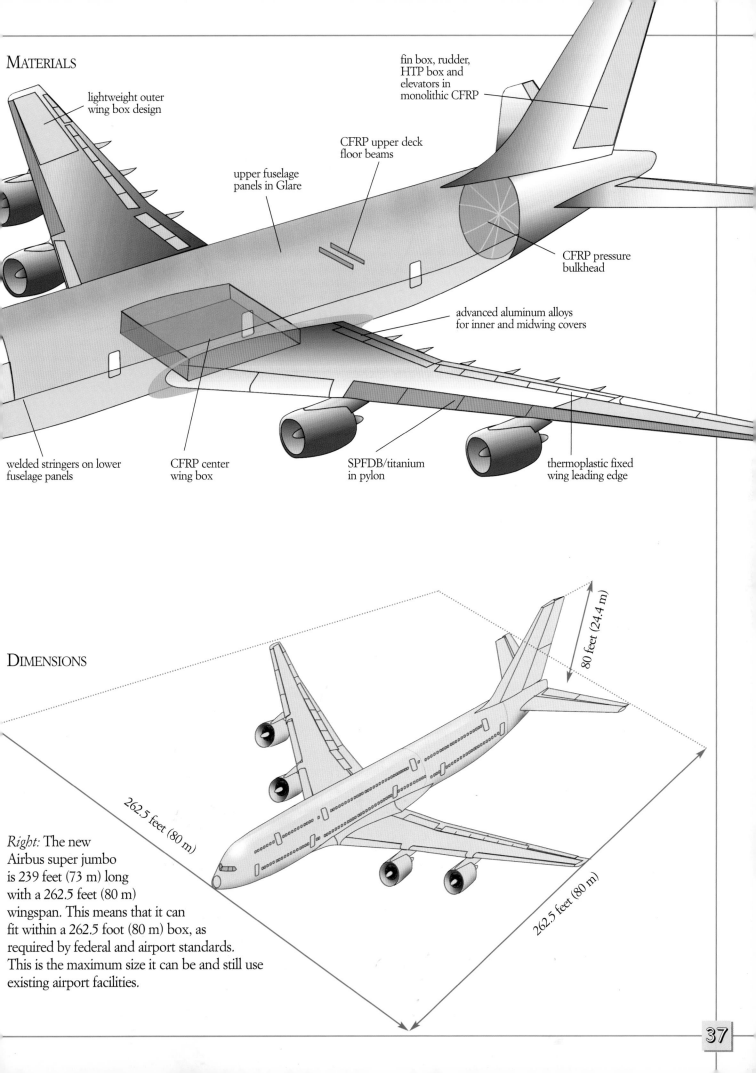

MATERIALS

lightweight outer
wing box design

fin box, rudder,
HTP box and
elevators in
monolithic CFRP

CFRP upper deck
floor beams

upper fuselage
panels in Glare

CFRP pressure
bulkhead

advanced aluminum alloys
for inner and midwing covers

welded stringers on lower
fuselage panels

CFRP center
wing box

SPFDB/titanium
in pylon

thermoplastic fixed
wing leading edge

DIMENSIONS

80 feet (24.4 m)

262.5 feet (80 m)

262.5 feet (80 m)

Right: The new
Airbus super jumbo
is 239 feet (73 m) long
with a 262.5 feet (80 m)
wingspan. This means that it can
fit within a 262.5 foot (80 m) box, as
required by federal and airport standards.
This is the maximum size it can be and still use
existing airport facilities.

The Interiors

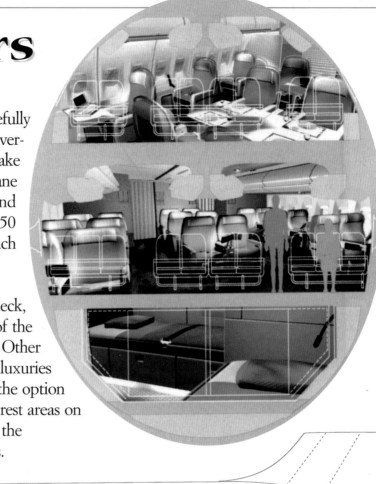

The inside of the super jumbo has been carefully planned also. Airbus designed the plane with several sets of exit and entrance doors, which will make boarding and getting off easy and fast. The plane will have two passenger decks: the main deck and the upper deck. The main deck will be almost 50 percent larger than the 747 passenger deck. Each Airbus A380 seat will have its own arm rests.

The A380 offers additional room on a lower deck, which is located beneath the main deck. Part of the lower deck will hold flight baggage and cargo. Other parts of the lower deck can be designed to offer luxuries to travelers. Airbus will give airline companies the option of including bars, business centers, libraries, or rest areas on the lower deck. Airbus designers will customize the lower deck to meet the individual airline's needs.

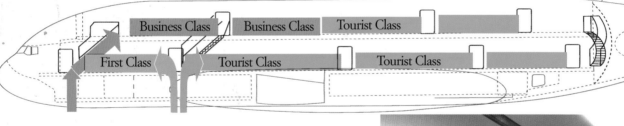

Business Class · Business Class · Tourist Class
First Class · Tourist Class · Tourist Class

Some airlines have expressed interest in having all economy cabins. Economy means that the seats are small and arranged closely together. This is so more passengers can fit on the plane. Other airliners have expressed interest in devoting a floor exclusively to high-paying customers, or first-class. The first class customers would have their own entrance and exit doors for the plane. First-class seats are larger than economy seats and are farther apart. Another seating choice is business class, where seats are larger than economy, but placed closer together than first-class seats.

According to Airbus, one airline has expressed interest in putting a casino on board. Whatever the airline companies demand, Airbus will try to deliver. Airbus representative Noel Foregard says that ultimately, these super jumbo planes will be like cruise ships in the sky.

These are just some of the interior designs proposed for the Airbus super jumbo jets. Airlines will be able to choose certain arrangements, such as luxury first class accomodations as seen above (top) and at left. They also plan to have wider aisles, entrance areas, and staircases, as seen just above.

The Future

The future of super jumbo jets remains to be seen. Airbus has made a guess about what kind of airplane future commercial aviation will require. Other companies like Boeing disagree about where the future will take us. They feel the future may lie in a smaller aircraft that flies faster at nearly the speed of sound. Other people have different ideas.

One particular new design idea has shown a great deal of promise. It's called the Blended Wing Body, or BWB. NASA is planning to fly a small BWB model to see if it will work. The model will be 35 feet (10.7 m) wide. It will be piloted using remote controls. Boeing is working with NASA on this project.

The BWB looks like one large wing. The body of the plane—where passengers sit—is blended into the wing. This creates a large, smooth surface. Its design will cut down on drag. The full-size version of the plane would be 67 feet (20.4 meters) wider than the 747. The wing span of a 747 is 211 feet, 5 inches (64.4 meters). This would not allow the plane to be used at existing airports and runways.

This design combines elements that the A380 and Sonic Cruiser have to offer. It would fly just below the speed of sound and it could carry more than 800 people. An added bonus is that the BWB would use less fuel than current jet planes and would actually be safer.

Ultimately, the designs of today and tomorrow's jet planes may lead us to space. During his administration, President Ronald Reagan asked that our government look into developing new supersonic jets. These jets would enter outer space at supersonic speed. They would orbit and then return to Earth. Such planes could be capable of going from New York to Tokyo in two hours. Traveling in such a way is called hyperspace transport.

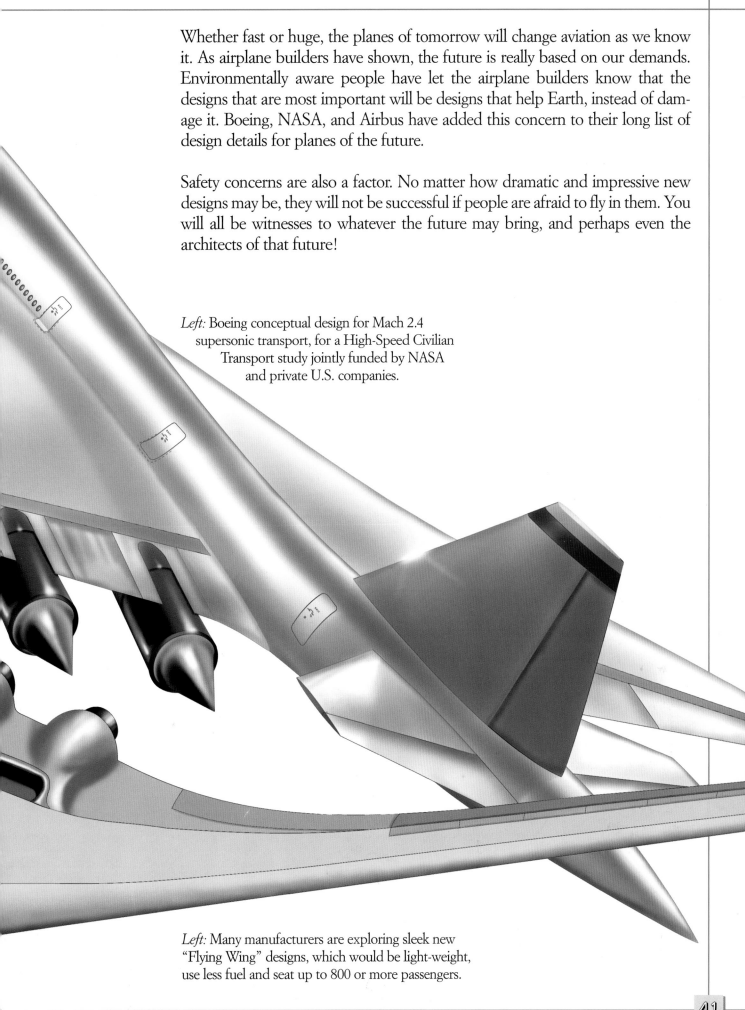

Whether fast or huge, the planes of tomorrow will change aviation as we know it. As airplane builders have shown, the future is really based on our demands. Environmentally aware people have let the airplane builders know that the designs that are most important will be designs that help Earth, instead of damage it. Boeing, NASA, and Airbus have added this concern to their long list of design details for planes of the future.

Safety concerns are also a factor. No matter how dramatic and impressive new designs may be, they will not be successful if people are afraid to fly in them. You will all be witnesses to whatever the future may bring, and perhaps even the architects of that future!

Left: Boeing conceptual design for Mach 2.4 supersonic transport, for a High-Speed Civilian Transport study jointly funded by NASA and private U.S. companies.

Left: Many manufacturers are exploring sleek new "Flying Wing" designs, which would be light-weight, use less fuel and seat up to 800 or more passengers.

Major Airlines of the World

There are countless airports and airliners all over the world. Whether they will change to accommodate ever larger and faster airplanes remains to be seen. For now, many will use the new Airbus super jumbo until it becomes clear that airline customers want or need something different from airline travel. This map could change drastically depending on whatever exciting new advances in technology the future may bring!

BRITISH AIRWAYS

Top Ten Very Large Aircraft Airports

In 2019, more than half of the world's fleet of 1,235 very large aircraft will be used on flights from just the top ten airports.

(The numbers in the red circles are the numbers of very large aircraft that operate from each airport.)

1 Moscow (NRT)	116
2 London (LHR)	96
3 Hong Kong (HKG)	83
4 Los Angeles (LAX)	74
5 Singapore (SIN)	56
6 New York (JFK)	50
7 Bangkok (BKK)	47
8 Frankfurt (FRA)	44
9 Taipei (TPE)	38
10 Sydney (SYD)	35

Anchorage *ANC*

Vancouver *YVR*
Chicago *ORD*
Indianapolis *IND*
Minneapolis *MSP*
Detroit *DTW*
Toronto *YYZ*
San Francisco *SFO, OAK*
Denver *DEN*
Atlanta *ATL*
New York *JFK, LO*
Washington *IAD*
Los Angeles *LAX*
Memphis *MEM*
Dallas *DFW, AFW*
Honolulu *HNL*
Orlando *MCO*
Miami *MIA*

Rio de Janeiro *GIG*
São Paulo *GRU, VCP*
Santiago *SCL*
Buenos Aire *EZE*

TWA

virgin atlantic *Virgin*

UNITED

ILF

AA **American Airlines**

AIR FRANCE

London
LHR, LGW

Amsterdam *AMS*
Frankfurt *FRA*
Paris
CDG, ORY
Munich *MUC*
Luxembourg *LUX*

Madrid
MAD

Rome
FCO

Moscow *NRT*

Nagoya
NGO, NGO II

Tokyo
NRT, HND

Sapporo *CTS, HKD*
Beijing *PEK*
Seoul *SEL II*

Fukuoka *FUK, KMQ*
Shanghai *SHAII*
Osaka
KIX, ITM
Kagoshima
KOJ, KMI

Delhi *DEL*
Okinawa *OKA*
Guangzhou *CANII*
Taipei *TPE*

Jeddah
JED
Dubai
DXB
Mumbai *BOM*

Hong Kong *HKG*

Bangkok *BKK, BKK II*
Manila *MNL, MNLII SFS*
Kuala Lumpur *KULII*
Singapore *SIN*

Jakarta *CGK*

Johannesburg *JNB*

Brisbane *BNE*

Sydney *SYD*   Auckland *AKL*
Melbourne *MEL*

According to Airbus the large, and
growing, populations in Asia mean that
three out of the four major markets for
larger aircraft will be in to and/or from
Asia: Trans-Pacific, Asia-Europe,
and within Asia.

Glossary

aerodynamics (ayr-uh-dy-NA-miks) The study of objects in motion in the air.

aero-engine (AR-oh-en-juhn) An engine used for flying.

aeronautics (ayr-oh-NAW-tiks) Science of flight.

afterburners (AF-tur-ber-ners) Devices built into the tailpipe of turbojet engines for injecting fuel into the hot exhaust gases and burning it to provide extra thrust.

ailerons (AY-luh-rahns) Movable sections on the edge of a wing.

altitude (AL-ti-tood) Height from the ground, measured in feet.

aviation (ay-vee-AY-shun) Air travel.

bogies (BOH-gee) Trucks or supporting frames for wheels.

cargo (KAHR-go) Goods or merchandise that is transported in a ship, a vehicle, or a plane.

cockpit (KAHK-pit) A space in a vehicle (boat, ship, or plane) from which the vehicle is piloted or steered.

compressor (kuhm-PREH-ser) The part of a jet engine that squeezes air.

combustion chamber (kuhm-BUHS-chun CHAYM-ber) A part of a jet engine that burns air and fuel.

drag (DRAG) A natural force that works against objects in motion.

FAA (Federal Aviation Administration) A government organization that governs the safety and security of air travel and aviation.

fuselage (fyoo-suh-LAHZH) The body of a plane.

empennage (ahm-puh-NAHZH) The tail end of a plane.

environmentally friendly (in-VY-ruhn-men-tuhl-ee FREN(D)-lee) A substance or thing that does not harm the environment.

freight (FRAYT) Goods to be shipped or transported; cargo.

Glare (GLAYR) A laminate made from alternating layers of aluminum and glass-fiber reinforced adhesive.

gravity (GRA-vih-tee) A natural force that attracts objects to Earth.

hangar (HAYNG-er) A large building that stores airplanes.

jumbo jet (JUHM-boh JET) The largest type of passenger plane.

laminate (LA-mih-net) Something made up of thin layers bound together by adhesive.

lift (LIFT) The force that pushes an object upward.

mach (MAHK) The speed of something in relation to the speed of sound.

meteorology (mee-tee-yer-RAH-luh-jee) Science of weather.

NASA (National Aeronautics and Space Administration) A government organization that researches Earth, space, and aviation science.

nacelle (nah-SEL) The outer casing of a jet engine.

navigation (na-vuh-GAY-shun) The method of plotting and maintaining a course of travel.

pitot tube (PEE-toh TOOB) A tube with a short angled bend that is placed vertically in moving fluid with the opening of the bent part of the tube facing into the flow. It is used to measure the speed of fluid flow.

port (PORT) The left side of a aircraft or ship when looking forward.

pulley (PUH-lee) A small wheel that provides lifting force through a system of ropes or chains.

ramjet (RAM-jet) A type of jet engine used for supersonic flight.

rivet (RIH-vet) A steel fastener with two rounded heads used to join pieces of steel or other metal.

rudder (RUH-der) A moveable surface that helps control the plane while in a turn.

spar (SPAHR) Any of the main members that run the length of an airplane's wing and carry the ribs.

starboard (STAR-bord) The right side of an aircraft or ship when one is looking forward.

static dischargers (STA-tik DIS-charj-ers) Elements on the wings of an airplane that release electricity.

super jumbo jet (SOO-per JUHM-boh JET) A plane that will be larger than the jumbo jet.

supersonic (soo-per-SAH-nik) Anything that can go above or faster than the speed of sound.

thrust (THRUHST) A force that moves an object forward.

turbine (TUR-byn) A part of a jet engine that powers the fan and compressor.

turbofan (TUR-boh-fan) A type of jet engine that uses a large fan to gather air.

turbojet (TUR-boh-jet) A type of jet engine that uses air and fuel to create thrust.

turboprop (TUR-boh-prahp) A type of jet engine that uses its power to turn a propeller.

turbulence (TUR-byuh-lens) Uneven flight due to weather conditions and winds.

undercarriage (UN-der-kar-ij) The landing gear of an airplane; or a supporting framework.

Additional Resources

Books

Bledsoe, Karen and Glen Bledsoe. *The Blue Angels: The U.S. Navy Flight Demonstration Squadron.* Mankato, MN: Capstone Press, 2001.

Butterfield, Moira and Spencer Davies (Editor). *Jets.* New York: Dorling Kindersley Publishing, Incorporated, 1996

Kent, Zachary. *Charles Lindbergh and the Spirit of St. Louis in American History.* Berkeley Heights, NJ: Enslow Publishers, 2001.

Kerrod, Robin. *Jet Airliners.* Danbury, CT: Franklin Watts, 1990.

Parr, Jan. *Amelia Earhart: First Lady of Flight.* Danbury, CT: Franklin Watts, 1997.

Robinson, Nick. *Super Simple Paper Airplanes: Step-by-Step Instructions to Make Paper Planes That Really Fly from a TRI-Plane to a Jet Fighter.* New York: Sterling Publishing Company Incorporated, 1998.

Sweetman, Bill. *Supersonic Fighters: The F-16 Fighting Falcons.* Mankato, MN: Capstone Press, 2001.

Taylor, Richard L. *The First Solo Transatlantic Flight: The Story of Charles Lindbergh and His Airplane, the Spirit of St. Louis.* Danbury, CT: Franklin Watts, 1995.

Web Sites

www.historicwings.com

www.nasa.gov/kids/kids_airplanes.html

www.pbs.org/kcet/chasingthesun

www.nasm.edu/nasm/NASMexh.html

www.women-in-aviation.com